Frank Shipsides' Bristol

Also by the artist

Bristol Impressions
Bristol: Profile of a City
Bristol: Maritime City

Frank Shipsides'
BRISTOL

with text compiled by John Sansom

REDCLIFFE
Bristol

First published in 1984 by
Redcliffe Press Ltd, Bristol

Dedicated to Phyl Shipsides and
her priceless diary which in the
creation of this book has been the
artist's salvation.

ISBN 0 905459 87 3

Printed in Great Britain by
Burleigh Press Ltd., Bristol

Contents

Foreword

I WAS very pleased to be asked to write a foreword to this book, and I consider it a great honour, as I have been an admirer of Frank Shipsides' work for more years than I care to remember.

Frank, a relative newcomer to the City, having come here from the North in the 1940s, has taught me to open my eyes to the beauty and the quirks of architecture that abound in our City, and I am sure this book will do the same for all its readers. He has a talent for being able, first to see, and then to record, the odd corners that even I as a Bristolian must have walked by many times but that have gone unnoticed.

The formal Georgian buildings, the unassuming brickwork of the dockside warehouses and the reflection of these in the waterways which are Bristol's trademark have been interpreted and captured in his own inimitable style.

He takes us along little known alleyways as well as the more familiar streets pointing out, in his vignettes, much that must be preserved for the citizens of the future.

We are indeed fortunate that we have in Frank Shipsides an artist who looks at our City with an appreciative eye – encouraging us all to do the same, and to value our unparalleled heritage.

Hubert Williams, 1984

The Making of an Artist

SOME YEARS after the first world war, a young apprentice designer in a Mansfield tin box manufactory was given the job of working on an advertisement depicting the famous Suspension Bridge at Clifton in Bristol.

'I had to do a painting from a photograph supplied by W.D. & H.O. Wills. It was to go on the lid of a cigarette tin,' recalls artist Frank Shipsides. 'I remember saying to myself, "this is magic, I'd love to see that bridge some day".'

Sixty years later, paintings of the Suspension Bridge and other landmarks lovingly depicted by one of Bristol's best known artists, adorn the walls of countless homes.

Frank Shipsides was born in Mansfield, where his father worked in the hosiery business. The unusual family name, which seems singularly appropriate for an artist renowned for his marine paintings, is said to have originated in the Nottinghamshire village of Gotham, of 'wise men' fame.

The family had mild artistic leanings; father was a good musician and Frank's elder sister had a stronger-than-average interest in art. Against this sympathetic background, Frank's headmaster effected an introduction to the studio manager in the artists' department at Barringer, Wallis & Manners. The embryo artist was fourteen years old, and about to embark on a seven years' apprenticeship.

'It was not terribly skilled work to begin with. We apprentices had to start early in the morning, mixing litho ink for the men, changing the water pots, making tea in the afternoons and fetching beer and snuff in the evenings. The most artistic thing I did in those early days was to dust down the potted palms and the busts on plinths which added tone to the studio.'

More responsible work came later, copying old masters for reproduction on chocolate and biscuit tins for the Christmas market. The seven years passed slowly, but agreeably. The studio manager was a martinet, but 'he looked after his apprentices,' recalls Frank Shipsides, 'and we had a good grounding in the business. Of course, the prospects were good. We could look forward to earning at least £4 a week when we were indentured, which was a lot more than most working men in those days.'

His apprenticeship behind him (and with it, the days of fetching and carrying), the young Frank Shipsides could call himself a fully fledged journeyman, working more or less on his own initiative.

A long spell at the Offset Process Company in Nottingham followed. This was a trade shop, proofing brochures, catalogues and show cards. 'It was a great experience. We worked like Hell. If you wanted to leave early, say at eight o'clock of an evening, you'd slip down the back stairs in case old Toddy saw you. At ten or eleven at night one of the kids would be waiting with a barrow while you were getting the last colour on, so he could rush the proofs to the last train to London, or wherever. Someone would be waiting at the other end to collect.

'Sometimes, on a Saturday, I'd look out of the window and see folk on their way to play tennis. Tennis! Our life was our work in those days.' There was little or no time, even, for one's own painting.

But Frank did have time for courting, and had been with Offset

The Wanderer, *immortalised by the poet, John Masefield, and seen entering Cumberland Basin: Windsor Terrace, on the heights of Clifton is in the background.*

about seven years when he married Phyllis Woods, a Mansfield lass who had been born within a stone's throw of the Centre Tree of Sherwood Forest. 'Who knows,' says Frank, 'maybe descended from Robin Hood and Maid Marian?' It seemed time for a change. 'I had always been interested in shipping and the sea, and had long had a hankering to live nearer ships. In those days, the great centres of printing were Nottingham, London (not so much the big stuff, more in the line of trade shops), Birmingham, Manchester and, of course, Bristol. Bristol, with E.S. & A. Robinson, Mardons, Bennetts, and so on, seemed the ideal combination of job prospects and the shipping which I wanted to paint.'

World war was imminent. Frank found a position in Bristol, with Bennetts, the printers, only to switch, to help the war effort, to a job as draughtsman with an associated engineering firm (he had been found medically unfit for the Forces). But his love affair with the city had begun.

After the war, he joined John Lees, and settled in Portishead for the sea views. In 1948, he moved over to Mardon, Son and Hall as a senior artist, and worked there for about twenty years. But his private work was growing: he was painting more and more and, to the point, selling as well.

In the meantime, Frank and Phyl had been bringing up a family; and a family with art in its blood. Daughter Jennifer worked as a restorer with Frost & Reed and is now on the conservation staff of the National Trust at Snowshill in Gloucestershire. Their son, Patrick, is a technical illustrator who paints marine subjects in his free time. He and his wife, Anna, a talented flower painter, run 'painting for pleasure' evening classes in Portishead.

Going freelance provided the balance between enough commercial work, as designer and retoucher, and his true love. After eighteen months, a chance meeting with Jim Fardon of the Alexander Gallery led to a first one-man show in the early nineteen seventies. Frank already had something of a following, and had joined Bristol Savages

Opposite and overleaf: *pages from the artist's sketchbook, 1946.*

REDCLIFFE
1946—

DETAILS OF WOODEN BARGE

DETAILS OF STEEL BARGE

GREY
RED

BRISTOL

GREY
BLACK

TOTTERDOWN

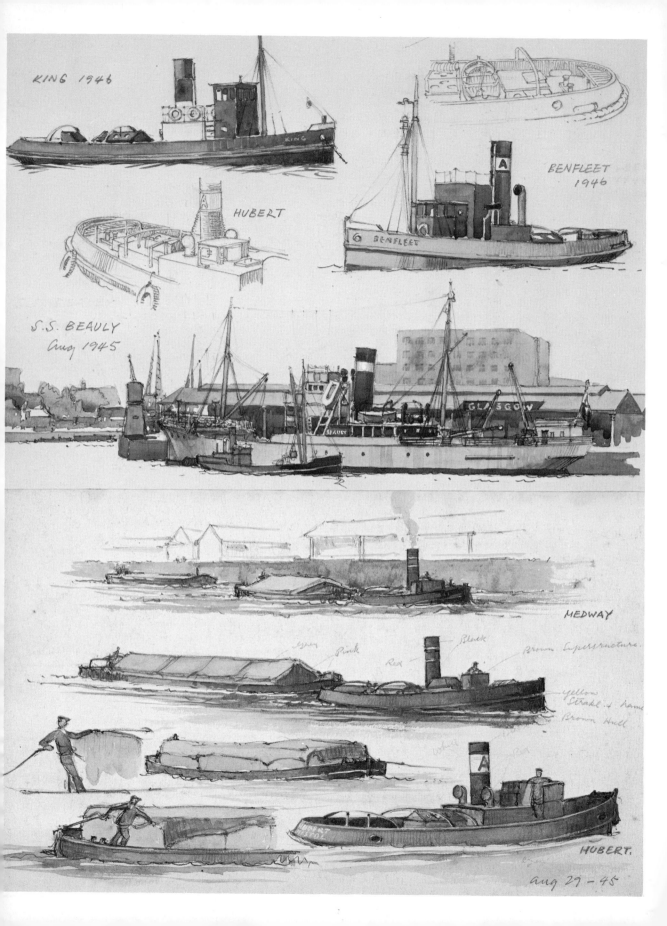

KING 1946

HUBERT

BENFLEET
1946

BENFLEET

S.S. BEAULY
Aug 1945

GLASGOW

BEAULY

MEDWAY

Grey   Pink   Red   Black   Brown Superstructure.

yellow
Strahl & name
Brown Hull

HUBERT.

Aug 27 - 45

a few years earlier at the invitation of Alfie Moores and Harold Packer.

That first show was almost a complete sell-out, and has been followed by another five even more successful exhibitions at the Alexander. These days, queues form on the pavement on Blackboy Hill on Shipsides preview nights, and within minutes of the doors opening, a gratifying rash of red stickers has spread throughout the gallery.

'I owe Alexander Gallery a great debt,' says Frank Shipsides. 'When they suggested an exhibition, I was thrilled, and worked hard to make it a success. I remember doing a particular painting of that scene that everyone loves: St. Mary Redcliffe Church looking up from Prince Street bridge, in a morning light, the spire silhouetted against the yellow sky. And I remember the gallery's partners asking what I thought it might fetch. I mentioned a figure, only to be told that two people had already offered to buy it at a price nearly three times what I thought it was worth.'

John Cleverdon, for the gallery, says 'It has been a pleasure to co-operate with Frank Shipsides in six shows, and to watch his development over the years.

'When he retired from commercial work, he was able to concentrate on capturing the "atmosphere" of his subject matter and take more time doing preparatory sketching on location. I think this has given his work, if anything, a greater freedom than it perhaps had before.

'Frank has established himself as an important topographical artist, and over the years he has made an impressive record of the face of the City and of its maritime past and present.'

FRANK SHIPSIDES ~ 1984 ~

The Artist at Work

IN TALKING to Frank Shipsides about art, one is soon aware of an enthusiasm which amounts not just to a love of painting, but also of the physical processes of putting paint on the canvas.

But even more than the satisfaction of seeing the finished work taking shape in the studio, he relishes the preliminaries. 'I find that a sketch book is a must, and the camera is a useful aid in the race against time. The camera can rarely capture atmosphere, though, which is so very important; for this, one has to rely on one's sketches, with colour notes – and on memory. A good memory is vital to an artist, both to recall detail, and to give a spark of spontaneity to the finished work. I like to do quite a lot from memory.

'I work in oil and watercolour. Oil enables one to put more depth into a picture, but I enjoy the discipline of working in watercolour. One cannot afford to make mistakes. Watercolour is a delicate art, greatly under-rated in my view.

'Composition seems to take care of itself, when you have found the right spot. I remember one occasion in Bruges when I had spent a lot

Corn Street, Bristol.

of time choosing just the right viewpoint, when a passer-by stopped to talk about the work in progress, commenting that Winston Churchill had painted from that very spot. I was not surprised. Any artist with a natural feel for composition would have come to the same conclusion.'

In choosing a subject, Frank Shipsides looks for beauty. Of course, this is a subjective matter. 'Some artists would enjoy painting a loaf of bread on a platter, and produce a lovely painting, but *I* need to feel an emotional response. It's difficult for me to get worked up about a bag of Mother's Pride.

'But Corn Street in a silvery evening light, that's another matter. Or a rusty old tramp steamer, a bit scruffy to look at, but full of character and romance. When I paint an old ship, it's not just what the eye sees, but also what I *feel* about her, about the cargoes she used to carry, and the men who worked on her over the years.'

In recent years, Frank Shipsides has had the opportunities he used to dream of as a young apprentice artist in Mansfield. His greatest love is to paint ships, and especially the square rigged vessels. His ship paintings are based on a detailed knowledge of how the ships actually worked, the precise detailing of sail and rigging. In the case of old ships long since broken up, he studies old photographs, plans and books.

His finished ship paintings, although far from being technical drawings, look authentic because they are accurate, even if the artist never saw the ship in real life. Authenticity is also aided by Frank's experience as a ship model maker. He was a keen member of the Bristol Ship Model Society, and his models have been displayed in the City Museum, and exhibited in London and Stockholm, where they were awarded silver and bronze medals.

The Tall Ships Race is a time of pilgrimage for the Shipsides. Frank talks of one particular outing to Dartmouth. 'We are approaching the town by that steep hill, with the Royal Naval College on the left, and the escape road running into the hillside. Ahead, across the tennis courts in Coronation Park, the river is full of ships' masts. It is a

The University Tower, seen across Berkeley Square.

16

FRANK SHIPSIDES—19

marvellous sight, with ships moored right up the river.

'I can hardly wait to park the car. A few quick sketches, with colour notes, juggling a bit with the compositions, but the finished picture will be authentic, believable.

'The morning light is perfect, with a little mist creating the impression of a stage set, the weak sun faintly dappling the water.

'The Race is about to start, and it's a rush to get the quick scribbles into the book, indicating positions, the flags they are flying, spots of colour to aid the composition. The wind is variable, so the ships move slowly, giving us time to move in and out of them, the *Malcolm Miller, Winston Churchill, Master Builder* and so on. By now, it is a top light, with the sun high in the sky. The roofs of the houses in the background are highlighted, the rest in shadow. These are magic conditions for painting.

'Light is an important ingredient in any painting. I have painted in the Mediterranean, but much prefer the subtler tones one gets at home. Whether the sun is low, casting long shadows, or in the mid-day sky, with soft shadow below the brilliantly lit roofs, or whether you are looking into light, seeing everything in silhouette, even commonplace objects achieve a rare beauty.

'One image sticks in my mind. It was the day of the Opening of the Royal Portbury Dock, and I was invited to the ceremony. This particular morning, the sun was shining through a slight mist, and the Royal Yacht appeared, the sun just lighting up her superstructure. The sky and sea seemed to merge, with the ship floating, suspended in the magic air.'

Although a dedicated artist, Frank Shipsides loves telling self-deflating stories. 'Any artist setting up easel at a beauty spot, or in the street, can expect to attract at least some interest from passers-by. One learns not to let it interfere with one's work. On one occasion, though, I was painting away in the centre of Bristol – it was an afternoon around half past four – and the crowd of onlookers seemed to be growing. At last, an elderly woman stepped forward,

An unusual view of Brandon Hill, with St. George's Church and the houses of Park Street.

19

presumably to voice a general admiration for my painting. "Excuse me", she said hesitantly, indicating the railings behind me, where hung a scruffy canvas bag, "but are the 3-Stars in yet?"

'On another occasion I was working on the quayside, feeling pretty pleased with the way things were going. And so, it seemed, were several bystanders, who thoughtfully had not come too close, for fear of disturbing the artist at work. They spoke in hushed tones, but not so hushed I could not hear them. "Look at that beautiful work," said one. "Yes", said another reverentially, "you can always recognise the professional touch, by the way they hold the brush." At this, with a flourish, I dropped more colour onto the picture, just to show they were not mistaken in their judgement, and glanced round with a nod and a smile. Three fellow artists from the Savages were standing there, with handkerchiefs to their mouths, laughing so much they nearly cried.'

By 1977, Frank Shipsides had long since acquired a loyal following, and had been offered a third one-man show by the Alexander Gallery. But in that year, his work was to take on a new dimension. He was approached by the publisher, John Sansom with an idea for a book about Bristol, with Frank Shipsides contributing fifty or sixty drawings.

'I was delighted, of course, but sceptical. Would people want to buy a book of pen-and-ink drawings?' The answer came in November, when the book, *Bristol Impressions,* was launched at the gallery, with an exhibition of the original drawings. Drawings and books sold like hot cakes. *Impressions* has been reprinted twice since then. In 1979, Frank Shipsides collaborated with the historian, Helena Eason on *Bristol: Profile of a City*. This was to be another best seller. Again published with a pre-Christmas exhibition, the new book sold even faster, with the last two copies being urgently delivered to a Clifton bookshop on Christmas Eve. A reprint early in the New Year sold out.

Would a third book fare as well? With Robert Wall, noted maritime and aeronautical writer, as his partner Frank set to work in

The Tall Ships Race, Dartmouth.

Above: *Welsh Back in its heyday: an evocative reconstruction commissioned by Bristol Chamber of Commerce & Industry.*

Right: *Another Shipsides' favourite: Broad Street on a quiet Autumn afternoon.*

22

1981 on the illustrations for the most ambitious title yet. *Bristol: Maritime City* showed that the Bristol public was ready for another happy blend of authoritative text and delightful illustration.

Altogether, the three books contain about two hundred paintings and drawings, making a unique record of the city's buildings and its maritime history.

Commissions for paintings, too, have played an important part in the artist's work. An invitation by the City Council to paint a series of fighting ships bearing the name 'Bristol' was a great honour.

The artist's meticulous attention to detail meant consulting many authorities on naval and historic detail and a visit, with Councillor Robert Wall, to Portsmouth to inspect recent modifications to the present ship.

The seven pictures depicting ships dating from 1653 to the missile destroyer of the present day now hang prominently in the main entrance to the Council House.

A further commission came, in 1984, when the City Council requested another painting to present to the captain and crew of the present *H.M.S. Bristol* at a Mansion House ceremony.

'Later that evening, we attended a reception on board the ship at Avonmouth,' recalls Frank Shipsides. 'The band of the Royal Marines, marching and counter-marching, was playing on the quay. As we watched and listened to that stirring music, we had a great feeling of pride in the City, and the ship bearing her name, and affection for the charming people we had met that day.'

King Street, Bristol.

25

A two-hour sketch done in the studio at Bristol Savages' 'Wigwam' in the Red Lodge: a nerve-wracking time for the artists who have to complete a painting of a subject nominated by the chairman for the evening. Eric Franklin, in the chair on this particular Wednesday evening in 1984, nominated the subject 'English', and is now the proud owner of Frank Shipsides' sketch.

26

Bristol Savages

FOR A STREET with George Oatley's monumental University Tower as a backdrop, Park Row is one of Bristol's least distinguished thoroughfares. But it has some interesting associations.

The Bristol artist, William Muller lived at the White Hart, as a plaque on the wall records. Not far from here used to stand the Princes Theatre, one of the greatest losses in the 1940 blitz, especially for Bristolians who can remember pre-war pantomime. The site is now blandly occupied by a petrol filling station, although some concession to local sentiment was made when adjoining blocks of flats were given theatrical names.

Park Row's finest building is the Red Lodge, on the corner of steep sloping Lodge Street. Its setting is demeaned by the concrete squalor of the nearby Trenchard Street multi-storey car park. Even so, this is one of Bristol's great treasures, its quiet, agreeably proportioned exterior giving no clue to the magnificent Elizabethan interior. It dates from 1590, and was a lodge to the Great House, owned by John Yonge who entertained Queen Elizabeth I there during her famous

Brandon Cottage: the home of Bristol Savages from 1907 to 1920.

visit to Bristol in 1574. The Great House survived until 1861; the site is now occupied by the Colston Hall.

The Red Lodge itself has an interesting history. In the nineteenth century, Dr James Cowles Pritchard lived here, writing *The Natural History of Man*. Mary Carpenter, a famous Victorian social reformer, ran a girls' reformatory at the Lodge from 1854 to 1877, and the school continued to operate until after the Great War.

Today, the Red Lodge is open to the public as one of the city's fine collection of museums.

It is also the home of Bristol Savages, that unique society which has contributed so much to the city's artistic life over the years.

As John Bedford, the Savages' honorary secretary, explained, the society started casually, as so many do, when a group of artist friends began to meet weekly to sketch and talk about painting. They met first in Ernest Ehlers' studio at Alfred Place in Kingsdown one autumn evening in 1894. They were congenial, pipe smoking but serious minded evenings with the artists sketching a subject nominated by the host. This was the start of the famous 'two hour'

*President Frank Shipsides
introducing Wednesday evening
guests.*

*The Savages' 'Wigwam'.
(photos: John Heming).*

sketches which are a feature of the Savages' Wednesday evenings to this day.

Their ambitions grew until, ten years after that tentative 'get together', the group formed itself into a formal society, holding its first meeting above a gunsmith's shop at 39 Corn Street, next door to the Commercial Rooms.

Before long, the Savages again needed more space, and took to renting a room at the Royal Hotel on College Green, until a more suitable and permanent 'wigwam' was established in 1907 at Brandon Cottage on Brandon Steep.

One story of those days is the occasion that Captain Scott attended the annual dinner. The Savages donated a sum of money towards his ill-fated Antarctic expedition. At their request, the money went to the purchase of a husky dog, to be named 'Brandon' after the Savages' headquarters.

The move to Red Lodge came in 1920. Mary Carpenter's old reformatory had closed, and the property was now on the market. James Fuller Eberle, to whom the Savages were already greatly indebted, and a group of friends, raised the money, with support from Sir George Wills. The old building was renovated, and a 'wigwam' in the form of an old tithe barn was built in the garden under the supervision of a Savages member, C. F. W. Dening, architect and author of books on the city's buildings.

The work done, the Red Lodge was offered as a gift to the City Council, subject to the Savages being allowed to use it as their headquarters. That happy arrangement still exists. There are about 450 members, and a long waiting list. Most are 'lay' members, who are designated as green feathers; blue feather members are the entertainers, and the red feather artist members represent the continuing link with those modest Kingsdown days. The full story is entertainingly told in Colston Waite's delightful booklet *The Story of Bristol Savages*.

The Savages are members of what is probably the oldest art club of its kind in the country. John Bedford aptly sums up the bond which unites members from many walks of life: 'a shared love of the arts,

Frank Shipsides,
President of Bristol Savages, 1983/84.

Artists at work in the Studio. Left to right: *Brian Lancaster, John Palmer, Alfred Moores and Frank Shipsides. (photo: John Heming).*

good conversation and a warm sense of comradeship with one's fellow beings. In short, the Savage spirit.'

The society's activities centre around the traditional Wednesday evening, with the artists painting their two-hour sketches in the studio before the other members arrive.

Frank Shipsides, a popular member and twice President, sums up the atmosphere at the two-hour sessions. 'You know the famous lines from the Henry Newbolt poem, "there's a breathless hush in the Close tonight"? The tension at the Clifton College playing fields on that famous night was nothing compared to the hush in the Savages' studio around 5.45 p.m. when the chairman for the session enters to chalk on the board the subject for the evening's sketch. His choice is met with groans all round. Where *do* they conjure up these impossible subjects?

Broad Street, from St. John's Arch.

A Sunday evening in the 1970s, full of nostalgia, saw the Flying Fox, *much loved R.N.V.R. training ship leave Bristol for the last time, on her way to the breakers' yard.*

34

'Somehow, we get through, and with the Chairman buying us all a beer, we begin to see there's some good in the chap after all.'

When finished, the sketches are displayed in the Wigwam for the rest of the members to view on their arrival, and to be wittily 'appraised' in public by a fellow artist.

There follows an evening of entertainment provided by the blue feathers; an evening of talent, good natured 'barracking' when the secretary reads the minutes, and a relaxed, friendly atmosphere for the Savages and their guests. The entertainment, of a remarkably high standard, varies from week to week. On a typical Wednesday, the audience might be regaled by a tenor, a conjuror and a string trio. It all adds up to a memorable evening.

An annual exhibition of Savages' paintings is held each Spring, opened by the Lord Mayor. It is always a popular event, with a high proportion of the paintings being sold.

Over the years, many notable people have been associated with the 'Wigwam'. The Doyle Carte Opera Company were frequent visitors. Members were honoured to have the late Duke of Beaufort as a member and patron, who used to attend the Wednesday evening sessions when time allowed. On one noted occasion, a small group of Savages were invited to Badminton House to give a royal performance for Her Majesty Queen Elizabeth and family.

The Wigwam is used, too, on occasion by various worthy organisations, such as The Antient Society of St. Stephens Ringers, founded in the reign of the first Queen Elizabeth and whose purpose in life is to raise funds for the upkeep of the fabric of the city's parish church.

Floating Harbour

FEW SIGHTS stir the Bristol imagination more than a tall masted sailing ship gliding up the Avon destined for the city docks. Such a visitor today will probably be making a courtesy call, perhaps to adorn the quayside during one of the city's water-festivals.

Artist Frank Shipsides hankers not only after the long lost days of sail, but of the more recent commercial traffic that gave Bristol its distinctive flavour. 'I used to love the bustle of the Scandinavian timber ships unloading their fragrant cargoes bang in the middle of the city, and the coastal traders bringing Guinness from Dublin, or maybe loaded with something as everyday as coal, but they were marvellous to paint – *real* ships, rusted, grimy, a bit smelly but carrying on a tradition stretching back hundreds of years.'

It is fascinating to listen to Frank Shipsides talking about the old ships, and household Bristol shipping names, like Ashmead, Brown, Campbells, Kings, Bristol Sand & Gravel, Mark Whitwill, Bristol

St. Mary Redcliffe: a rare Shipsides' interior.

FRANK SHIPSIDES - 1984 -

38

Steam Navigation and, of course, Charles Hill. He was there to witness the launching, in July, 1976, of the *Miranda Guinness,* the last ship to be built in Bristol. 'It was an emotional moment for everyone there,' he recalls, 'truly the end of an era.'

'I also remember spending a day sketching, taking photographs, measuring, on board the *Annan* when she was moored at Belfast Shed, on St. Augustine's Reach. She was one of the marvellous Sloan Line ships. They were like great Edwardian yachts, with lovely lines and heavily raked masts and funnels.

'I was told one of the sister ships, the *Findhorn* had mosaic laid on her main deck, with Italian workmen brought over to do the work.

'There were still several of the big 'four masters' around after the war. I remember the *Passat* at Avonmouth, but they've all gone now, apart from the *Padua* which the Russians bought and converted into a cadet training ship. They have made a wonderful job of her, and under her new name of *Kruzenshtern,* she is a regular in the Tall Ships Races.'

Nothing can properly replace the working docks and their vanished commercial traffic, with its whiff of foreign places, but after standing idle for years Bristol city docks are undergoing an exciting sea change. Faintly echoing the past, a flourishing boat float adjoins the s.s. *Great Britain,* which is one of the focal points of the waterway; and downstream are two new housing schemes, at Rownham Mead and Baltic Wharf, where houses have replaced the timber drying sheds which stood here for a hundred years or more.

Sailing dinghies, wind surfers, pleasure craft and busy ferryboats now contribute to a lively kaleidoscope of activity in this stretch of the Floating Harbour.

To the east of the *Great Britain,* work has started on the Bristol Maritime Heritage Centre. A specially designed new building will house the Hillhouse and Hill Collections, a unique heritage of ships' plans, models, paintings and documents accumulated over centuries by the famous Bristol shipbuilding firm of Charles Hill.

The Maine, *a German visitor to Narrow Quay.*

Between here and Prince Street Bridge are the city's expanding Industrial Museum, augmented in the summer of 1984 by a Port of Bristol section, and the National Lifeboat Museum on the site of William Patterson's yard, from which Brunel's *Great Western* was launched in 1837.

Facing Prince's Wharf, and thrusting into the Centre, is St. Augustine's Reach which could be said to epitomise the rebirth of the Floating Harbour. For here are the former sheds which now house

Watershed: bringing people back to the waterfront.

the Exhibition Centre, where the International Wine Festival is held each year, Radio West and Watershed, a unique media and communications centre devoted to film, video and photography.

Opposite the Exhibition Centre is Bush House, a massive grey pennant stone warehouse built to house tea from China and now home to Arnolfini. This early conversion, in the 1970s, showed the doubters just what could be done to bring new life into the docks.

The City Docks full of life during the International Wine Fair.

But things are happening everywhere in the docks these days. Restored and new houses in Bathurst Basin have achieved national recognition; the Welsh Back has been refurbished and tree-planted, and by Bristol Bridge new office buildings bring back a sense of scale to a sadly decayed stretch of water.

If half the proposed improvements are carried through, Bristol in five years' time will be a very exciting place indeed.

One of the key events in the saga of the city docks was the return of the s.s. *Great Britain.* Frank Shipsides, Bristol's marine artist *par excellence,* almost missed it. The ship was due to be brought up the river from Avonmouth on the evening of Saturday, July 18th, 1970. That very evening, St. Ursula Players were staging an invitation show at Bristol's Little Theatre, following their success in winning the South West Drama Rose Bowl presented by the *Evening Post.* As honorary patrons, Frank and Phyllis Shipsides would want, above all else, to be present for that.

Happily, an ill-wind forced the postponement of the last leg of the old ship's historic journey until the Sunday morning. 'So I was able, thank God, to witness her return after all. I must have been the only person in Bristol to welcome the delay. Sunday morning dawned and I didn't quite know what to expect. I think everyone was surprised by the fantastic turn out. Half of Bristol seemed to be lining the Portway and the Clifton heights. The excitement, the emotion, was terrific. The crowds were cheering, some shouting "Keep her". It's hard to credit now, but there was still a question mark over the ship's future.

'She came slowly, tantalisingly into view, towed proudly by *Sea Alert,* one of King's tugs, with the Cory tug *Falgarth* astern. Geoffrey Palmer, the Lord Mayor, was there in the leading launch, looking as happy as a sandboy. We all were. Nobody who was there will ever forget that day.

'I took as many photographs as I could – there was no time for sketches – to try to capture all the cavalcade.'

H.M.S. Bristol *at Avonmouth in 1983.*

Captain Gordon Walwyn of H.M.S. Bristol with Frank Shipsides after the Lord Mayor, Councillor Claude Draper had presented the ship's portrait to the captain in the summer of 1984.

Those images were to form the basis of many different versions of the *Great Britain*. Buyers included merchant bankers Antony Gibbs & Co, which once owned the ship itself.

Painting the return of Brunel's masterpiece led the artist to depict more Bristol scenes; he undertook more commissions, too. One challenge was to 'reconstruct' the *Matthew* in which Cabot crossed the Atlantic to discover Newfoundland nearly 500 years ago. 'Of course, no one knows precisely what she looked like, although we have a good idea of the construction of a typical merchant ship of the time. Several models have been made, but the late Norman Poole, an old friend and colleague of mine at Mardons, is generally reckoned to have got as near as anyone could to the original. He assumed the ship was 50–70 tons, about 70 feet long, with three masts. I based my painting very much on his research.'

The painting hangs in the Council House on College Green and can be seen at any time the council offices are open. There is also to be a statue to Cabot on the quayside outside Arnolfini. All this activity reflects the growing civic pride in Bristol's heritage.

John Cabot's achievement is commemorated elsewhere in the city. On Brandon Hill, Cabot Tower was erected in 1897–98, to a design by W. V. Gough, to mark the 400th anniversary of the historic voyage. There is also a plaque, by Neptune's statue at the head of St. Augustine's Reach and, atop the nearby Bristol & West extension building, a gilded 'Matthew' weathervane glints in the summer sun. Away to the east, John Cabot and Sebastian are depicted in a stained glass window in St. Mary Redcliffe.

One of the earliest, and certainly the most colourful, reconstructions of the Cabot story hangs in St. Nicholas Museum. Ernest Board's large canvas, painted in 1906, depicts the navigator's departure from an imaginary quayside in Bristol. It is a great favourite, although there are critics of its historical details.

A Thames barge at the International Wine Fair, 1984.

An emotional day for Bristol: the return of s.s. Great Britain, *in 1970, with another Brunel masterpiece in the background. The Clifton Suspension Bridge had not been built when the great ship left Bristol in 1844.*

The City Restored

STILL THE most beautiful city in England, said Sir John Betjeman of Bristol some years ago. He would be even more enthusiastic about the city today.

But Bristol came close to being turned into another Birmingham. It suffered badly between the 1950s and the early 1970s, when developers, encouraged by the city's planners, vied with each in the number of old buildings they could destroy, and in the mediocre replacements they inflicted on a long suffering city.

The legacy of those years is to be seen in uninspired, badly weathered office blocks throughout the historic heart of the city. In Broadmead, desperate attempts to 'landscape' some character into the spaces between the multiple stores have been only partly successful. The handful of survivors of the planners' postwar blitz catch the eye like rare gems. On the bright side, recent new buildings in the area are of an altogether higher standard and give hope for the future.

In 1975, Colin Amery and Dan Cruikshank highlighted some of Bristol's buildings then under immediate threat. It was a depressing

47

Lodge Street, derelict for many years, now imaginatively restored, with new housing behind.

list: Lodge Street, Brunswick Square, superb town houses in Prince Street, and a nearby seed warehouse, Boyces' Buildings in Clifton, the bottom of Christmas Steps, houses on St. Michael's Hill. Old Market was falling apart. Ashton Court Mansion had only just been reprieved. The Outer Circuit Road seemed destined to cut great swathes through old streets, houses and the city docks. The future of the waterway itself was bleak.

Modest eighteenth century housing on the Kingsdown slopes had been swept away to make room for 14-storey slabs; no one in authority had apparently seen that this was a precious piece of townscape appropriate to its setting and harmonious in its scale.

Ten years have seen a complete transformation. By the mid-1970s public opinion, through Bristol Civic Society, and more localised pressure groups, was making itself heard. A new breed of planners, putting people before roads, were beginning to reverse the process and to put Bristol back together again.

In 1977, Bristol City Council, with Historic Buildings Council support, started a five year restoration programme which was to be

Bristol Cathedral.

The former Tramway Offices on the Centre, superbly and authentically rebuilt.

hailed as the most successful urban conservation scheme in the country. The good work continues today.

The City's achievement rekindled a pride in Bristol's architectural heritage which rubbed off onto the developers. New buildings are of a much superior quality to those of ten years ago, even though a conservative public opinion has not warmed to everything new, and whole areas have been coaxed back to vigorous life.

Remarkably, Bristol has more 'listed' Georgian buildings than Bath, and altogether over 3,600 buildings are designated, and protected, because of special historical or architectural interest.

Some notable rescues stand out. As Frank Shipsides' drawings show, the Christmas Steps area is now a joy to visit; more than an efficient exercise in restoration, the St. Bartholomew's development has created an exciting new environment and provided small, human scale offices.

In 1980, Lodge Street, long since derelict, was used as a lurid cover illustration for *The Fight for Bristol,* a sustained piece of polemic from the Civic Society about the destruction of much of old Bristol. By

51

Bathurst Basin: restored and new houses on the waterfront, and in walking distance of the City's theatres, restaurants and galleries.

1984, beautifully restored and again housing families right in the City Centre, this unassuming terrace was featured in a Bristol Marketing Board brochure.

Brunswick Square, and surrounding streets, are an exciting mix of restoration and new buildings, providing for office use and, crucially, for housing.

Elsewhere, the rebuilding continues. Old Market is being pulled together. Here Bristolians owe a debt to Dorothy Brown's Visual and Environmental Group for their pioneering work. New housing is being built on the waterfront at Hotwells and in Bathurst Basin. Important buildings, and sometimes complete streets, have been saved throughout the City. It is a great success story, and truly a City Restored.

A magnificent restoration scheme, at the bottom of Christmas Steps, recreates the intimacy of this medieval corner of the old city.

'Horse and Rider' a life-size bronze statue by local sculptor David Backhouse, in an open courtyard at St. Bartholomew's.

Opposite: Colston Street, at the top of Christmas Steps, rescued from the dereliction which was threatening the whole area.

— FRANK SHIPSIDES — 1984 —

FRANK SHIPSIDES — 1984 —

55

Bristol Bridge looking better than it has for nearly fifty years. The Welsh Back quayside, restored and tree-planted; the growing Castle Green on the site of the ruined city centre; and new offices bringing life and dignity back to the area.

One of the few buildings in Broadmead to escape the planners' post-war blitz.

'The Ornament of Bristol'

FEW MEN have had a greater influence on Bristol than Isambard Kingdom Brunel, the city's favourite, if adopted, Victorian son. More than one hundred years after his death, his works have inspired some of Frank Shipsides' most memorable paintings.

It all started more than fifty years before Brunel's birth, when a wealthy Bristol wine merchant, William Vick, bequeathed a sum of money for a bridge to span the Avon Gorge between Clifton and Leigh Woods.

The story is well known. When the legacy had grown to £8,000 a design competition was held by the Merchant Venturers. As a young man of 23 Brunel submitted four of the 22 designs, all of which were rejected by Thomas Telford, doyen of civil engineers who had been appointed to judge the competition. Brunel's proposed bridges had spans of up to 916 feet, and were dismissed by Telford as potentially unsafe.

After Telford's own subsequent proposals were turned down because of cost, Brunel succeeded in a second competition, held in

1830, largely by reducing the span to 630 feet. That scheme, with Egyptian detailing, was later modified, but work started in 1831.

At the turf cutting ceremony, Sir Abraham Elton prophesied that the young engineer would be hailed throughout the land for having 'reared that stupendous work, the ornament of Bristol and the wonder of the age.'

Sadly, Brunel's recognition, as far as the Clifton Suspension Bridge was concerned, was to be posthumous. Money ran out, legal problems arose and economic activity in the city was disrupted by the fearful Bristol riots.

After a fresh start in 1836, work proceeded for a few years until a second cash crisis forced the abandonment of the project in 1843, with the two support piers completed, but a yawning gap between them.

Another £30,000 was needed. It was not until 1861, two years after Brunel's death, that a new company was formed with sufficient capital to see the project through to completion. The bridge was finished three years later, and officially opened on December 8th, 1864.

Sir Abraham Elton had been right. The elegant bridge is Bristol's most famous monument, firmly on the tourist's itinerary, and lazily thronged with strolling families and couples on warm summer evenings. How many million camera shutters have clicked to capture its silk-spun simplicity or, illuminated at night, that gap-toothed silhouette on a velvet sky?

The young Brunel's decision to enter the bridge competition gave Bristol not one masterpiece, but several. Those early visits brought him into contact with the local business fraternity, and he was to be involved with the city for more than twenty years. He was not a Bristolian, but more than once expressed the wish to be considered one.

Isambard was still only 26 when, in 1833, the backers of the proposed London to Bristol railway system invited him to act as their engineer. The immense task of surveying the 120 mile route was carried out with breathtaking speed, work started after the passing of

Sculptor John Doubleday's portrait in bronze of Isambard Kingdom Brunel on Broad Quay. Commercially-inspired statues are springing up like mushrooms throughout the city. Recent and planned commissions include equestrian groups at Brunel House and St. Bartholomews, Sabrina on Narrow Quay, four groups depicting the seasons at Baltic Wharf, and another Doubleday statue, at the Phoenix Assurance offices, in addition to the City's own commission of a statue of John Cabot near the Arnolfini.

= FRANK SHIPSIDES - 1984 -

the Great Western Railway Bill in 1835 and astonishingly the rail link between the two cities was completed by 1841. This was one of Brunel's outstanding achievements and, as Angus Buchanan and Michael Williams make clear in *Brunel's Bristol,* it was inspired largely by Bristol enterprise and Bristol capital.

The present Temple Meads Station was built in the 1860s to a design by Sir Matthew Digby Wyatt, but Brunel's original terminus remains more or less intact. It is the oldest railway terminus in the world to retain its essential features, and is designated a Grade I listed building of national importance. For years the splendid shed, with immense mock hammerbeam roof, has languished as a covered car park. A dignified future, however, is now assured. British Rail has carried out major repairs, with Historic Buildings Council grants, and leased the terminus to the Brunel Engineering Centre Trust for renovation and refurbishment. The Trust is seeking appropriate new uses for this historic building.

Frank Shipsides' drawing shows the neo-Tudor facade fronting Temple Way. The ticket office at the front had three floors. On the first floor is the original board room, scene of many a stormy meeting in the formative years of the GWR. When restoration is complete, Bristolians will be able to appreciate the full grandeur of Brunel's Temple Meads. Proposals for the sympathetic redevelopment of the area, if fully realised, will one day provide a proper setting.

On Wednesday, May 26th, 1982, Bristol and London shared a unique occasion: the unveiling of two larger-than-life statues to the great Victorian engineer. At Paddington Railway Station, the Lord Mayor of Westminster pulled the cord on a statue by John Doubleday of a seated Brunel, after Andrew Breach, chairman of Bristol & West Building Society had formally presented it to British Rail in the person of Leslie Lloyd, General Manager of British Rail, Western Region.

After travelling by a scheduled high-speed Inter-City 125 train to Bristol, Andrew Breach was soon afterwards inviting Councillor George Maggs, Lord Mayor of Bristol to perform the second unveiling of the day. The Bristol statue, outside the extension to the

The main facade of Brunel's Temple Meads. Passengers, arriving by foot or coach, would enter through the arch on the left. The building is now being restored.

63

Bristol & West's Head Office at Broad Quay, is a standing figure looking towards the waterfront. The statue was given by the Society to the people of Bristol to mark both Brunel's and Bristol & West's long associations with the city.

To see another Brunel masterpiece, the visitor might board a ferry boat a stone's throw from the Broad Quay statue, and make for the Albion Dockyard less than a mile downstream.

Here, in its original dry dock is the s.s. *Great Britain,* in 1970 lovingly towed 7,000 miles from its Sparrow Cove graveyard in the Falklands, back through cheering crowds to the very spot from which she had been launched 127 years earlier.

Since then, restoration has proceeded steadily, transforming a rusting hulk into something approaching her former glory. Since 1970, countless people have passed through the turnstiles to walk around this historic vessel, once the height of passenger comfort, in its day the largest ship ever built and the first ocean-going ship to be built of iron and screw-propelled.

The saga of the *Great Britain's* return has a symbolic quality. Some City Fathers were sceptical. They saw on the pontoon not a born-again chunk of Bristol history, but a truncated white elephant that threatened to be a drag on the city's exchequer. But vision prevailed, in a sense marking Bristol's rediscovery of itself, a pride in an illustrious past and a growing confidence in the future.

The *Great Britain* was the second of Brunel's great ships to be built in Bristol shipyards. In 1837, a timber-hulled paddle steamer had been launched from William Patterson's yard, on what is now the site of the National Lifeboat Museum. The s.s. *Great Western* represented, in a tangible form, Brunel's breathtaking proposal to extend the railway from Bristol to New York by ship.

The ship proved an enormous success, although by the early 1840s she was trading out of Liverpool rather than Bristol.

The London-Bristol-New York concept has left us with another reminder of those heady days: Brunel House, behind the Council House, has long been a run-down office block (and was for some years a Turkish bath) but has recently been sympathetically restored.

Brunel House: once the Royal Western Hotel catering for stopping-over travellers from London to New York, now restored and used as offices.

As the Royal Western Hotel, it was built in 1837–39 by the architect, R. S. Pope working in collaboration with the engineer.

After the journey from Paddington, passengers bound for New York spent the night at the hotel before embarking on the *Great Western* for the transatlantic crossing. This transit service was short lived, and the building operated as a hotel for less than twenty years.

CAROUSEL

BRISTOL CATHOLIC PLAYERS Present

PRINCESS · IDA

• By W. S. GILBERT and A. SULLIVA

NEWMAN HALL   May 3rd to 15th, 1971

BRISTOL CATHOLIC PLAYERS

Present

TRIAL by JURY

And

The PIRATES of PENZANCE ·

by W. S. GILBERT & A. SULLIVAN

BRISTOL CATHOLIC PLAYERS

present H·M·S **'PINAFORE'**

by W. S. Gilb & A. Sullivan

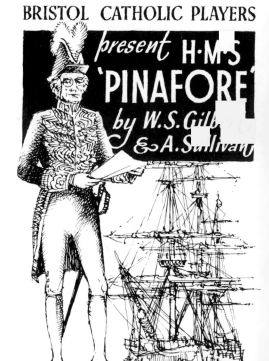

SOUVENIR PROGRAMME · MAY 1982

The PAJAMA GAME

ROYAL HOTEL   APRIL 22nd, 1966

NEWMAN HALL

An Artist in the Theatre

FRANK SHIPSIDES' interest in the life of the city extends to the theatre. 'Bristol could hardly have a better combination than the Hippodrome, with its enormous auditorium and stage large enough to take the great touring productions, and the Theatre Royal, smaller scale and intimate. We are the envy of many cities elsewhere in the country.'

A visit to the ballet at the Hippodrome was always a double delight for the Shipsides. 'There was the magic of the performance itself, especially if someone like Fonteyn was dancing and, of course, the sheer beauty of some of those superb sets. Our greatest love is the musical show, and we used to enjoy immensely the colourful Julian Slade productions like *Christmas in King Street* and *Salad Days*.'

But theatre for Frank Shipsides means not only the professional stage. Bristol has a tradition of flourishing amateur companies putting on first class productions. 'We became associated with the Bristol Musical Comedy Club years ago, when our friends and neighbours, the late Dennis Blower and his wife Mary were playing leading roles in their productions. That was at the time of the great Rodgers and Hammerstein spectaculars, among others, and with Jimmy Morris producing, the shows were always absolutely splendid. We were also members, with Mary and Dennis, of the Playgoers Club, principally a play-reading society, but with an annual production. I used to help with the sets.

'We have many friends, too, in the St. Ursula's Players, a marvellous company which has won numerous awards over the years. The dedication of people like Marie O'Sullivan, secretary, actress and producer, and Peter Woolston, their energetic chairman, is marvellous'.

Frank, who with Phyllis is an honorary patron, has designed and painted several sets for St. Ursula's, including *The Rape of the Belt*, *She Stoops to Conquer* and *Present Laughter*.

His connection with the Catholic Players goes back over thirty years. 'Two very good friends, Sid and Ailsa O'Connor took us to Knowle to look around the club of the Church of Christ the King. That was our first meeting with Monsignor Joseph Buckley, who was then parish priest of the church, in Filwood Broadway. He was forming a group of players, with young people very much in mind.

'The first venture was to be Gilbert and Sullivan's *Mikado*. Would I like to help? I gladly produced a design for the programme cover and did scale drawings for the scenery, which was painted by Father Buckley himself and Ted Marsh, one of the founder members. Although I only designed that first set, I've found myself designing *and* painting ever since.

'At the time, the Doyle Carte company were in America. They had heard of our humble production through Monsignor Buckley, and on our opening night sent a telegram: "From Broadway, New York to Filwood Broadway, Bristol, England, wishing you every success".'

When Monsignor Buckley was transferred to the Church of the Sacred Heart at Westbury on Trym, the Newman Hall was built,

"I have a song to sing-O". Jack Darlison as Jack Point in a Catholic Players' production of Gilbert and Sullivan's Yeomen of the Guard.

68

with a splendid stage and lighting equipment. It has been the venue for both the Catholic Players and St. Ursula's Players since 1962. With the Catholic Players specialising (but not exclusively) in Gilbert and Sullivan, Frank painted a large mural in the Newman Hall bar, depicting various characters from the operas.

'At one time, there was nowhere to store the sets, so we used to paint out and start again for the next production. Fortunately, Phyl and I love the involvement. My wife used to help with costume at one time, and with fittings required, and with me working on the designs, the house in Florence Park was sometimes like bedlam. We were especially busy during *Ruddigore,* as the second act required full length portraits for the transformation scene in the picture gallery and which I painted from the actual players in their costumes.

'It has been a very happy company to work with. Several members have been involved since the early days. Adrian Anglin, who is secretary and treasurer and assists with production; Jack Darlison, a great character actor; Jerry Summerell, the electrician who came to mend a fuse and has been in charge of lighting ever since. His wife, Kay, is wardrobe mistress.'

In 1984, the company gave a concert at Knowle to celebrate the fiftieth anniversary of the building of the estate. It happened to coincide with the Shipsides' golden wedding year. 'Somehow this leaked out, and after the concert, everyone was invited to the home of Connie Morgan, the pianist, whose husband, Trevor was a stalwart of the company for many years. Monsignor Buckley announced there were two occasions to celebrate. One was sad, as Phillip Cousins, the Vicar of St. Peter's and wife Janet, both members of the company for some years were off to Egypt, where Philip had been appointed Provost of Cairo Cathedral. The happy event, of course, was ours.

Top: *this painting of a scene from* Hadrian VII *was presented to Adrian Anglin, a pioneer member of the Catholic Players, to mark the company's 25th anniversary. He is shown with Don Morgan, who played the part of Hadrian VII.*

Bottom: *the artist's sketch for Act II of* Pirates of Penzance, *by courtesy of Gerry Summerell. It was another 25th anniversary presentation.*

'It is pleasant to look back over old friendships. There were those two marvellous men, Jack Clee, the writer of verse, and John Coe, critic and man of theatre.

'It has been a great honour to Phyl and myself to be made vice-presidents of the company, with Donald Adams, the great Gilbert and Sullivan singer, and his wife Muriel, who was a leading soprano with Doyle Carte.

'So we remember the chorus in the finale of the *Gondoliers:*
> "So goodbye Cachucha, Fandango, Bolero –
> We'll dance a farewell to that measure –
> Old Xeres, adieu – Manzanilla – Montero –
> We leave you with feelings of pleasure".'

TOWN and COUNTRY

Royal York Crescent, Clifton.

Christchurch, Clifton.

Top: *Campbell's paddle steamer,* Britannia, *one of the fleet's most popular ships with trippers between the wars. Here seen in the Bristol Channel with* Archibald Russell.

Bottom: *a four-masted barque passing Pill.*

Frenchay Church.

A typical Bristol scene: Tom Silvey's sand dredger, Sand Diamond *in Cumberland Basin. One of the last working boats in the City Docks, she was formerly the Scandinavian* Frierfjord *before being converted to her present use.*

Above: *West front of Bristol Cathedral.*

Top left: *the tranquillity of Saltford Lock, only a few miles from the centre of Bristol.*

Left: *The 'Jolly Cobblers': instant 'olde worlde' character in King Street.*

Top: *a romantic view of the truncated Clevedon Pier. With Government aid, Sir John Betjeman's favourite pier is to be fully restored.*

Bottom: *moving out at the start of the Tall Ships Race, Falmouth, 1982. Pictured is the* Dar Mlodziezy, *a newly built Polish full-rigger racing for the first time.*